RECREATE SCIENTIFIC DISCOVERIES

RECREATE DISCOVERIES ABOUT
SOUND

CRABTREE
PUBLISHING COMPANY
WWW.CRABTREEBOOKS.COM

ANNA CLAYBOURNE

RECREATE SCiENTiFiC DISCOVERIES

Author:
Anna Claybourne
Editorial director:
Kathy Middleton
Editors:
Sarah Silver
Elizabeth DiEmanuele
Proofreader:
Wendy Scavuzzo
Interior design:
Eoin Norton & Katherine Berti
Cover design:
Katherine Berti
Photo research:
Diana Morris
Print and production coordinator:
Katherine Berti

Images:
All images by Eoin Norton for Wayland except the following:
Dreamstime: Blue Ring Media: p. 5t
Getty Images: Hulton Archive: p. 10cl
Jones River Village Historical Society and the Kingston Public Library Local
    History Room: p. 26tr
Kym Maxwell: p. 22tr, 22cl
M Watts-Hughes. The Eidophone Voice Figures, 1904: p. 18cl, 19br
Shutterstock: front cover (spring toy, megaphone, speaker, record, stationery),
    p. 4tr, 5c (ultrasound), 7b, 11br, 17br, 24br, 29br
    Ana Aguirre Perez: p. 11bl
    Asier Romero: p. 15br
    Fabio Da Paola/REX: p. 6tr
    Goran Bogicevic: p. 5bl
    La Gorda: p. 5br
    Nejron Photo: p. 25b
    rawcaptured photography: p. 21br
    shu2260: p. 4cr
    Stock-Vector Sale: p. 29tr
Wikimedia Commons: p. 8tr
    Cornelis Bloemaert 1665. Germanisches Nationalmuseum/PD: p. 14tr
    Gilbert H. Grosvenor Collection, Library of Congress/PD: p. 5cr
    kndynt2099. cc-by-sa-2.0: p. 12cl
    Matthew Brady 1878. LOC: p. 20cl
    office museum/PD: p. 8cl
    Staats Sächsische Landesbibliothek und Universitåtbibliothek
        Dresden/PD: p. 14cl
    U.S. Navy photo by Photographer's Mate Airman Matthew Clayborne: p. 9bl
    US Patent Office/PD: p. 16tl, 26cl
University Archives, Kenneth Spencer Research Library, University of
    Kansas Libraries: p. 16tr
Every attempt has been made to clear copyright. Should there be any
inadvertent omission please apply to the publisher for rectification.

Library and Archives Canada Cataloguing in Publication

Claybourne, Anna, author
        Recreate discoveries about sound / Anna Claybourne.

(Recreate scientific discoveries)
Includes index.
Issued in print and electronic formats.
ISBN 978-0-7787-5054-3 (hardcover).--
ISBN 978-0-7787-5067-3 (softcover).--
ISBN 978-1-4271-2153-0 (HTML)

        1. Sound--Experiments--Juvenile literature. I. Title.

QC226.6.C533 2018   j534.078   C2018-902455-0
                                                                C2018-902456-9

Library of Congress Cataloging-in-Publication Data

Names: Claybourne, Anna, author.
Title: Recreate discoveries about sound / Anna Claybourne.
Description: New York, New York : Crabtree Publishing, 2019. |
    Series: Recreate scientific discoveries | Includes index.
Identifiers: LCCN 2018021346 (print) | LCCN 2018023779 (ebook) |
    ISBN 9781427121530 (Electronic) |
    ISBN 9780778750543 (hardcover) |
    ISBN 9780778750673 (pbk.)
Subjects: LCSH: Sound--Experiments--Juvenile literature. |
    Science--Experiments--Juvenile literature.
Classification: LCC QC225.5 (ebook) | LCC QC225.5 .C556 2019 (print) |
    DDC 534.078--dc23
LC record available at https://lccn.loc.gov/2018021346

Crabtree Publishing Company

www.crabtreebooks.com   1-800-387-7650

Published in 2019 by Crabtree Publishing Company

First published in Great Britain in 2018 by Wayland
Copyright © Hodder and Stoughton, 2018

Published in Canada
Crabtree Publishing
616 Welland Ave.
St. Catharines, Ontario
L2M 5V6

Published in the United States
Crabtree Publishing
PMB 59051
350 Fifth Avenue, 59th Floor
New York, New York 10118

Note:
In preparation of this book, all due care has been exercised with regard to the
instructions, activities and techniques depicted. The publishers regret that
they can accept no liability for any loss or injury sustained. Always follow the
manufacturers' advice when using electric and battery-powered appliances.

The website addresses (URLs) included in this book were valid at the time of
going to press. It is possible that some addresses may have changed or sites may
have changed or closed down since publication. While the author and publishers
regret any inconvenience this may cause to the readers, no responsibility for
any such changes can be accepted by either the author or the publishers.

Printed in the U.S.A./082018/CG20180601

CONTENTS

4 **Understanding sound**

6 **Found sounds** | Science: sound is movement, vibration

8 **Talk to the tube** | Science: carrying sound vibrations over distance

10 **It came from outer space!** | Science: using vibrations, pitch to make sound

12 **Bottle train** | Science: music and pitch

14 **Turn it up!** | Science: amplification and speakers

16 **Underwater ear** | Science: sound vibrations in water

18 **Seeing sounds** | Science: resonance patterns

20 **Get into the groove** | Science: recording and playback of sound vibrations

22 **Sonic sculpture** | Science: sound as art

26 **Intruder alert!** | Science: electric sound buzzers and circuits

30 **Glossary**

31 **Further information**

32 **Index**

TAKE CARE!

These projects can be made with everyday objects, materials, and tools that you can find at home, or in a supermarket, hobby store, or DIY store. Some projects involve working with things that are sharp, breakable, or need extra strength to operate. Make sure you have an adult to supervise and help with anything that could be dangerous. Always get permission before you try out any of the projects.

UNDERSTANDING SOUND

Sound is a big part of most people's lives. Like many animals, humans use sound to talk and share ideas.

You're almost always surrounded by sound. Music, singing, and dancing are a big part of our culture. Many inventions also use sound, including musical instruments, alarms, sirens, and phones.

WHAT IS SOUND?

Sound is a form of **energy**, like light, heat, electricity, or movement. When objects move back and forth, they create **vibrations** that push **molecules** into the air. This creates **sound waves**.

We hear sounds because of sound waves. Our ears turn sound waves into signals that get sent to the brain. The brain then reads and understands them.

THAT'S A BELL RINGING...

All the sounds we hear are vibrations. Each vibration is different. The speed of the vibrations decides how high or low a sound is. The strength of the vibrations decides the **volume** of a sound.

Sound waves can also travel through liquids and solids. For example, many fish can hear underwater.

1. Person hits drum

2. Drum **vibrates**

3. Sound waves move through the air

4. Sound waves enter ear and hit eardrum

5. Eardrum vibrates and vibrations spread inside ear

6. Vibrations send a signal to the brain

4

SOUND INVENTIONS

We have been able to record sound since the 1870s. Recording and playing back sounds is now an important part of our lives. Telephones, TVs, games, alarm clocks, and movies are inventions that use sound.

Sound is more than entertainment. Some inventions use sound to locate objects. There are also hospital machines that use sound to look inside the body.

Dolphins make clicking sounds underwater and listen to the echoes that bounce back off objects. This helps them find food.

*These pictures of a baby during the mother's pregnancy were created using **ultrasound**.*

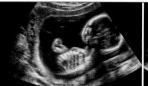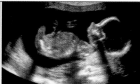

GOOD VIBRATIONS

When you hear lots of noises together, your ears take in different vibrations. For example, think of music. There might be different instruments and people singing all at the same time.

We can also feel sounds with other parts of our bodies, such as when we hear **loudspeakers**. Some animals even feel vibrations through the ground.

Inventor Alexander Graham Bell tests an early telephone. This telephone joined two cities, New York and Chicago, in 1892.

SONIC ART

Sonic art is art that makes sound. It is more than 100 years old!

Artists can create strange sounds with computers, called sound effects. These sounds are used in games and movies.

FOUND SOUNDS

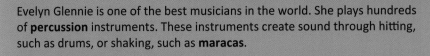

Make your own musical instruments, like Evelyn Glennie.

> *Anything you strike, anything you shake or rattle, or just anything that can be picked up, and you can create a sound.*
> *— Evelyn Glennie*

DAME EVELYN GLENNIE

(1965–)

Evelyn Glennie is one of the best musicians in the world. She plays hundreds of **percussion** instruments. These instruments create sound through hitting, such as drums, or shaking, such as **maracas**.

Evelyn also makes her own instruments with everyday objects she finds, such as farm tools. She has been deaf since the age of 12.

WHAT YOU NEED

- a strong wooden or cardboard box, such as a shoe box
- scissors
- thick felt or craft foam
- glue

- everyday objects from home, especially metal utensils and tools, such as: forks and spoons, metal bottle opener, wrench, bolts and screws, scissors, small pipes or tubes

1

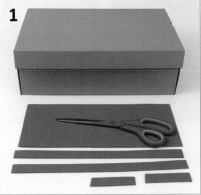

Step 1

Cut strips of felt or foam about 0.5 inches (1 cm) wide and a little longer than the box. If your felt or foam isn't long enough, join the strips together to make them the right length.

2

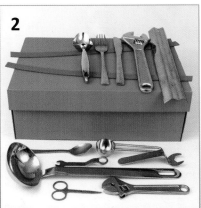

Step 2

Arrange the felt or foam strips on top of the box in a rough V shape. Lie each object across the strips, with shorter objects at the narrower end. Move the strips if needed so the objects don't touch the box.

3

4

5

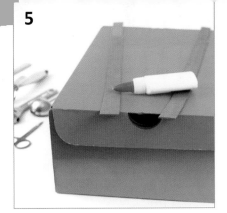

Step 3

Tap each object with another metal object, such as a spoon. Listen to the notes each one makes. Arrange them with the lowest note at one end and the highest at the other.

Step 4

If you don't like an object's sound, you can leave it out. You can also try moving it around slightly or hitting it in a different place.

Step 5

When you're happy with your instrument, take the objects off. Make sure you keep them in the right order. Glue the felt or foam strips in place and put the objects back on.

6

Step 6

You can play your instrument using one or two spoons. You can give it a name, too.

BANGING AND SHAKING

Percussion instruments involve hitting an object. This makes the object move and vibrate.

When you use objects of different sizes, you can make different notes. Faster vibrations make a higher note, and slower vibrations make a lower note. The smaller an object is, the faster it vibrates.

We call the highness or lowness of a sound the **pitch**. Each instrument has its own sound, depending on the shape and material.

Evelyn Glennie is deaf, but she can play music by feeling the vibrations of percussion instruments. She plays barefoot to feel the vibrations in the ground.

TALK TO THE TUBE

Link two different rooms or floors in your home with sound!

This officer worker in 1903 has four speaking tubes to use at the end of his desk.

JEAN-BAPTISTE BIOT

(1774–1862)

Jean-Baptiste Biot was a French math professor and space scientist. He was also a balloonist and inventor. In the early 1800s, he tried using long tubes to carry sounds. Tubes of even 0.6214 miles (1 km) moved sound from one end of the tube to the other.

People called these *speaking tubes*. Before telephones, speaking tubes helped people share messages on ships and in homes.

WHAT YOU NEED

- 16.5 feet (5 m) or more of corrugated plastic tubing, about 1.2 inches (3 cm) in diameter
- two large plastic bottles
- scissors
- strong packing tape or duct tape
- string or zip ties (optional)

1

2

3

Step 1

With an adult to help, cut the tops off both the bottles. Cut at the point where the sides of the bottle start to straighten out.

Step 2

With the help of an adult, wrap tape around the cut edges of the bottles. Cover up any sharp bits to make them safer to use.

Step 3

Attach the openings of the two bottles to the ends of the tube. You may be able to push or twist them together. If not, wrap tape around the openings to join them.

4

Step 4

Arrange the tube so that the ends are in two different rooms or parts of a house. You can then talk to another person by speaking into the tube while they listen at the other end. Even whispering is easy to hear!

You can use speaking tubes to link two bedrooms. You can also connect the downstairs of a house to the upstairs. Then you and your family can talk without changing rooms.

Ask an adult to help you to fix the tube in place. They can secure them by attaching the tube to bannisters or other objects with string or zip ties.

DOWN THE TUBE

When you speak into a tube, your voice makes the air inside it vibrate. The tube contains the vibrations and helps the sound travel farther. The bottles at the end of the tubes hold the sound waves so that they stay in the tube. This makes the sound louder when you listen on the other end.

Speaking tubes are still used today on some boats, such as this US Navy ship.

9

IT CAME FROM OUTER SPACE!

If you've ever wondered how sci-fi sound effects are made, try this!

Sound effects for radio and TV were created using a variety of equipment at the BBC Radiophonic Workshop in London, UK.

DELIA DERBYSHIRE

(1937–2001)

Delia Derbyshire was a musician and composer in the 1960s and 1970s. She worked at the BBC Radiophonic Workshop, where she made music and sound effects for TV and radio. She recorded voices, animal noises, and sounds.

Delia used everyday objects to make her sounds. She used objects such as lamps and bottles. Then she edited the sounds with equipment. She's most famous for creating the sounds used in the theme music for the TV show *Dr Who*.

" Any sound can be made into a radiophonic sound...The sort of sounds we usually use are electronic sounds of various sorts, and also sounds that are recorded, picked up by a **microphone**, everyday sounds and also musical instruments.
– Delia Derbyshire

WHAT YOU NEED

- a large metal spring
- two paper cups
- strong packing tape or duct tape
- sharp scissors
- spoons, chopsticks, or other objects for hitting the spring
- two people

Step 1

Turn a paper cup upside down so that you can see the rim around the base. With an adult, use the point of a scissor blade to make two holes in the rim, right next to the base of the cup. Do the same with the other cup.

Step 2

Take one end of the spring and thread it through the holes in one of the cups, so that the metal lies flat against the base. Tape the spring to the base. Attach the other cup to the other end of the spring in the same way, resting it on a table or fixed surface.

Step 3

Hold one of the cups and have another person hold the other cup. Pull the cups away from each other so that the spring slightly stretches. Now put your ear to the cup and gently tap the spring with a spoon or other object.

Step 4

Try using the device to make your voice sound alien and spooky, too. Speak or sing into your cup while the other person puts their cup to their ear. Then try it the other way around!

CHANGING VIBRATIONS

When sound travels along the spring, it moves and changes. This movement creates different vibration speeds. We call this change in vibration *speed frequencies*.

The sound moves along the spring into the cups. The sound can seem out of this world or alien.

If you have an audio editing app, such as WavePad, Audacity, or Hokusai, you could record the sounds and try making more changes to them, as Delia Derbyshire did.

BOTTLE TRAIN

Make a musical instrument that's played by a speeding train.

An AKB48 team singing and performing on stage

AKB48

(Formed in 2005)

AKB48 is a singing and dancing girl group from Japan. There are up to 120 members. They play concerts in smaller groups.

In 2016, the group released a video that showed a train playing music. The train zoomed past rows of bottles and hit them with drumsticks. The song was the famous *William Tell Overture*.

WHAT YOU NEED

- at least 10 empty glass bottles, as similar as possible in size and shape
- a toy train and tracks with sloping sections
- a chopstick or wooden craft stick
- two small metal bolts
- elastic bands
- tape
- a jug of water
- a metal spoon

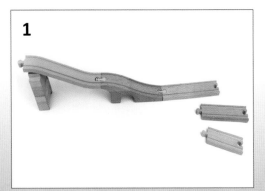

1

Step 1

Set up your train tracks to make a straight track that runs downhill. Put it on a hard floor with plenty of space around it.

Step 2

Use tape to attach one bolt to each end of the stick. One bolt will hit the bottles while the other acts as a balance.

2

3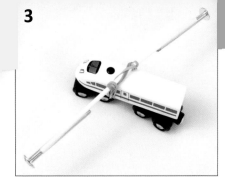

4

5

Step 3

Attach the stick to the top of the toy train using elastic bands. Make sure they don't touch the wheels. The stick should be at an angle.

Step 4

Add the bottles. Arrange them along one side of the track. Then position them so that the backwards-pointing end of the stick will hit them as it passes by.

Step 5

Pour different amounts of water into the bottles. This gives each bottle a different pitch (note) when hit. Test the sound by hitting the bottles with a spoon. Place the bottles so that they play a simple tune when struck in order.

Step 6

Put the bottles close together to make the notes play faster. Move the bottles apart to leave gaps between notes.

Step 7

To play the tune, put the train at the start of the track and start it moving. You may need to adjust the bottles to make it work better.

6&7

If you don't have a train and tracks, you can use a toy car or other vehicle. Make a simple track using a long strip of card stock with the sides folded up.

Do you have a battery-powered train? You could use this instead, on a length of flat track or a circle.

SELF-PLAYING INSTRUMENTS

Automatic instruments play a tune by themselves. They have been around since ancient times. The bottle train is an automatic instrument that works by moving at a steady speed to hit the bottles.

How does it work? The water slows down the speed of the vibrations in the glass. More water means a slower vibration speed. This means that the more water a bottle contains, the lower its pitch will be. This is how you can create different notes and music.

This wind-up musical box is an automatic instrument.

TURN IT UP!

Use the flared shape of paper cups to make phone speakers.

One of Kircher's creations

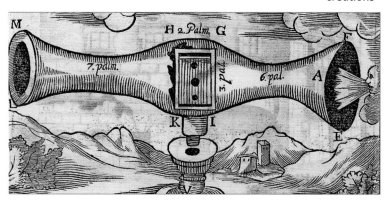

WHAT YOU NEED

- a smartphone
- an empty paper towel tube
- two paper or plastic cups (the bigger the better)
- scissors
- a marker
- two tissue papers or napkins

Step 1

Hold the bottom of the phone along the paper towel tube, right in the middle. Make sure this is the long side of the phone. Draw around the phone with the marker. With an adult to help, cut out the shape of the phone inside the line, using the scissors.

Step 2

Hold one end of the tube against the side of one of the cups, close to its base. Draw around the tube onto the cup.

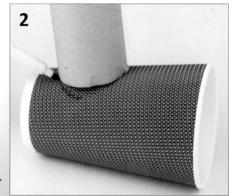

3

Step 3

With an adult to help, use the scissors to cut out the circle. Remember, cut just inside the line for a close fit. Now do the same thing again with the other cup.

4

Step 4

Gently crumple up the two tissue papers. If they have layers, separate them and use one layer. Push one tissue into each end of the tube. This helps to soak up very high-pitched sounds.

5

Step 5

Fit the paper towel tube into the holes in the cups. The cups should point in the same direction. Twist the tube so the phone-shaped hole is pointing up.

6

Step 6

Now switch the cell phone on and play some music. Push the phone down into the hole in the tube. The speakers will amplify the music!

PASSING IT ON

The sound vibrations from the phone speaker move through the tube into the paper cups. As the cups vibrate, they make the air vibrate, too. This sends sound waves out toward the listener.

The music is louder because the cups point the sound waves in one direction. Without the tube, sound waves move all over the room.

Horn-shaped speakers help amplify sound. This is why they are used at events.

15

UNDERWATER EAR

Is anyone there?

It can be hard to hear what's going on underwater, unless you have a **hydrophone**!

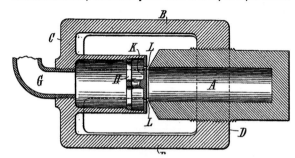

One of Blake's ideas for an underwater listening device

LUCIEN I. BLAKE

(1853–1916)

American Lucien I. Blake was one of the first people to create the hydrophone in the 1880s. This is a device that can hear underwater sounds. Blake had the idea after swimming in a lake. He heard sounds from a far distance.

Ships used hydrophones to hear signals from lighthouses and other ships. These signals helped them avoid crashes. People soon used them to listen to animals underwater. Biologists still use them today.

WHAT YOU NEED

- flexible plastic tubing, about 3 ft (1 m) long and 1 inch (2.5 cm) in diameter
- two funnels
- a balloon
- scissors
- strong packing tape or duct tape
- a bathtub or kiddie pool
- windup bath toys, jugs, spoons, or other noisy waterproof objects

Step 1

First blow up your balloon to stretch it. Then release the air. Lie the balloon flat and cut off the opening, just above the neck.

2

Step 2

Stretch the remaining part of the balloon over the wider opening of one of the funnels. Stretch the balloon as tightly as possible. This is tricky with a very big funnel. If you have two funnels in different sizes, choose the smaller one. You may need an adult to help.

3

Step 3

Push the two funnels into the two ends of the tube. If they don't fit, use strong tape to join the funnel and the tube together.

4

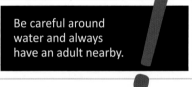

Step 4

Fill the bathtub or kiddie pool halfway with water. Put the end of the tube under the water. The balloon-covered funnel should be the side underwater. Listen at the other end.

5&6

Step 5

Ask someone to make noises in the water. For example, they can hit two spoons together or put a windup toy in the water.

Step 6

Listen with just your ears, then with the hydrophone. Can you hear a difference?

> Be careful around water and always have an adult nearby.

SOUND WAVES IN WATER

Humans use their ears to pick up sound waves. Sound waves from humans spread through the air, which is a form of gas.

Sound waves can also travel through liquids and solids. In fact, they travel faster through water because water is **denser** than air. This means the molecules that make water are closer together.

Our ears don't hear very well underwater. We hear better in air.

A hydrophone can help us hear underwater. It collects sound wave vibrations and transfers them into air. This can happen through a vibrating **membrane** (the stretched balloon). The balloon makes it easier to hear the underwater sounds.

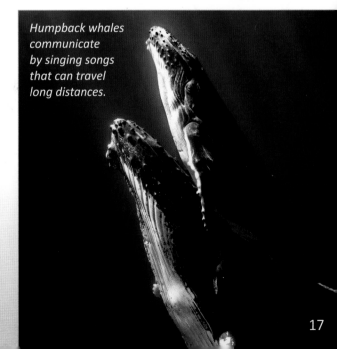

Humpback whales communicate by singing songs that can travel long distances.

SEEING SOUNDS

Build a machine that turns your singing voice into beautiful patterns!

One of the patterns Megan Watts Hughes made with her eidophone

Different versions of the eidophone

MEGAN WATTS HUGHES

(1842–1907)

Megan Watts Hughes was a Welsh singer and composer. While practicing her singing, she created a way to see each note. She used the sound waves from her voice to make a sheet of rubber vibrate. The sheet had a layer of powder, sand, water, or milk on it. As she sang, the objects turned into amazing flower-shaped patterns.

Megan named her invention the *eidophone*. She described the patterns as "voice-figures" or "voice-flowers."

WHAT YOU NEED

- a clean, empty, cylinder-shaped cardboard container, with a plastic lid
- scissors
- a craft knife
- a pencil
- a balloon
- a small funnel
- a plastic tube about 1 inch (2.5 cm) in diameter
- duct tape
- fine glitter

1

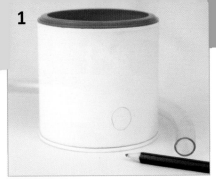

Step 1

Use tape to attach the funnel to one end of the tube. Hold the other end of the tube against the container near the base. Draw around it with the pencil.

2

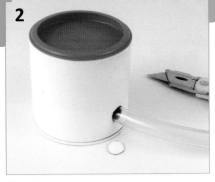

Step 2

Ask an adult to carefully cut out the circle using the craft knife. Check the tube fits into the hole. There should be a little space to spare to let air out when you sing into it.

3

Step 3

Take the lid off the container. Trace the pencil around on top of it to draw a circle on the lid, right inside the rim. Ask an adult to use a craft knife to cut out this circle, too.

4

Step 4

Blow up the balloon to stretch it. Release the air, then lie it flat. Use the scissors to cut off the open end, right below the neck. Stretch the balloon over the open top of the container and pull it tight.

5

Step 5

Take the lid with the hole cut in it. Push it back onto the container to hold the balloon in place. Wrap tape around the edge to put the lid, balloon, and container together.

6

Step 6

Sprinkle a thin layer of glitter onto the flat balloon surface. Fit the tube into the hole in the side of the container. Put the funnel end to your mouth.

7

Step 7

Sing a long, single note into the funnel. Higher notes work best. Each note helps the glitter make a different pattern.

WAVE VIBRATIONS

The eidophone's patterns happen because of the vibrations of the thin surface. The vibrations of the surface create **standing waves**. This causes the object on the lid to move. Parts of the lid move up and other parts of the lid move down. The patterns are the shape of the waves.

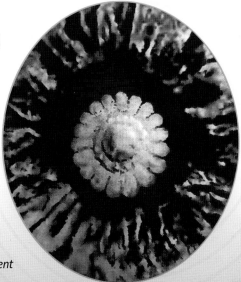

Megan Watts Hughes created different patterns by using many sounds.

GET INTO THE GROOVE

This record player shows how sounds are stored in a record's grooves.

A photograph, taken in 1878, shows Edison with an early phonograph.

THOMAS EDISON

(1847–1931)

Thomas Edison worked on many inventions, such as the lightbulb and film camera.

In 1877, he invented the **phonograph**. This was the first machine that could record and play back sound. The phonograph collected sound vibrations. Using a needle, it made a pattern on a spinning disk made of tin foil. Records replaced the disk years later.

Now there are many ways to record sound, including the computer. Records are still popular because of their sound quality.

WHAT YOU NEED

- a piece of card stock 8.5 x 11 inches (21.5 x 28 cm)
- a piece of paper 11 x 17 inches (28 x 43 cm)
- a thin, sharp needle or pin
- tape
- scissors
- two paperback novels, the same thickness
- enough felt to cover the front covers of both books
- four paper clips or binder clips
- a **vinyl LP record** (should have a very small hole in the center) that you don't mind getting scratched
- a pencil that fits tightly through the record's hole

If you don't have a vinyl record to use, you can probably find one at a thrift store, such as Goodwill.

1

Step 1

Take the large sheet of paper and curl it around to make a cone shape. The cone should close at the narrow end. Add tape to hold it in place.

2

Step 2

With the help of an adult, push the pin or needle through the cone, about 1 inch (2.5 cm) in from the pointed end. It should stick up at a right angle.

3

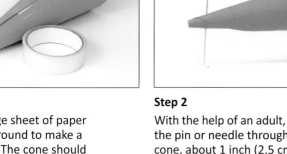

Step 3

Fold the piece of card stock in half. Cut a large semicircle shape out of the folded side. Make a fold along the two edges of the card. This will be a stand for the cone to rest in.

4

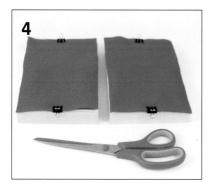

Step 4

Put the two books flat on a table with a space between them. Cut two pieces of felt to fit on top of each book. Use the clips to hold the felt in place.

5

Step 5

Push the pencil through the middle of the record and stand it up between the books. The pencil should rest on the table with the record resting on the felt. This will help you keep the record flat as you turn it.

6

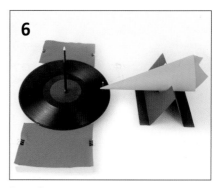

Step 6

Put the cone and its stand next to the record. Carefully place the tip of the pin or needle on the record, angled like the picture above.

7

Step 7

Rotate the record clockwise as steadily as you can, using both hands to turn the pencil. Once you have a normal speed, you should be able to hear the record playing through the cone. It may take some practice.

STORED VIBRATIONS

A record has a long spiral pattern running around the disc until it reaches the center. Sound waves make the needle vibrate. The needle then scratches patterns onto the record. When you run a needle through it again, these patterns make the same sound vibrations. The vibrations pass into the cone. This makes the sound easier to hear.

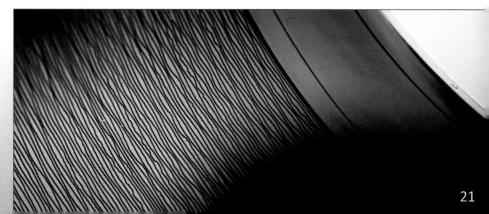

SONIC SCULPTURE

Create your own sound art installation.

Kym Maxwell and Dirk Leuschner's work Marble Run 2: The Materials are Listening, *2013.*

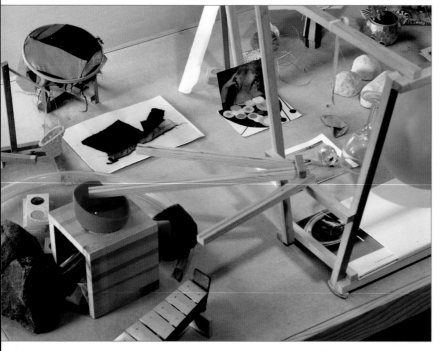

KYM MAXWELL

(1972–)

DIRK LEUSCHNER

(1962–)

Kym Maxwell is an Australian artist and teacher. She often works with children to make art. She worked with furniture maker Dirk Leuschner to create an art **installation** that makes sounds when marbles move through it. This is an example of sound art or sonic art, which is art that makes noises for the audience to hear. Sound art can be a sculpture with parts that move and vibrate. It can also be art that plays back recordings of sound.

WHAT YOU NEED

- a selection of objects to use to build the marble run and make sounds, such as: card stock, funnel, plastic and metal tubes, paper cups, springs, nails, wooden skewers, bells, balloons, paper clips, aluminum foil plates, old CDs, pliers, cutlery, metal wire, coins, buttons, metal washers, xylophone

- a large cardboard box
- tape
- scissors
- marbles
- paper towel roll
- duct tape

1&2

Step 1

Cut the largest side off your cardboard box to use as a base for your marble run. Lean it up against a wall or table to make a sloping surface or tape it to another box as a support.

Step 2

Attach sections and stages to the box for the marbles to run down. To fit as many in as possible, it helps to make each stage run across the box, from one side to the other.

> You can experiment with different ways to move the marbles and make sounds. These next steps are just ideas. You can come up with your own, as well.

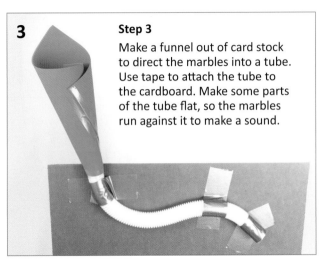

Step 3

Make a funnel out of card stock to direct the marbles into a tube. Use tape to attach the tube to the cardboard. Make some parts of the tube flat, so the marbles run against it to make a sound.

Step 4

Cut the neck off a balloon. Stretch the large section over a funnel to create a drum for the marbles. Curve thick card stock around the drum to catch and redirect the marbles.

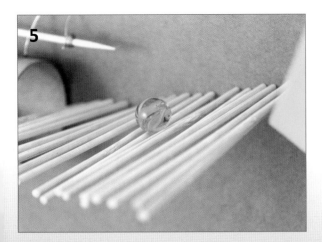

Step 5

Push a row of toothpicks or skewers into the cardboard base to make a path.

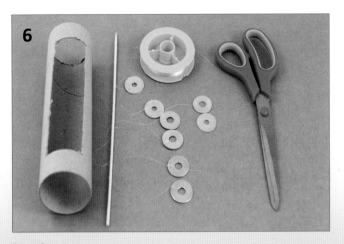

Step 6

Cut a cardboard tube open. Use thread to hang small metal objects for the marbles to hit.

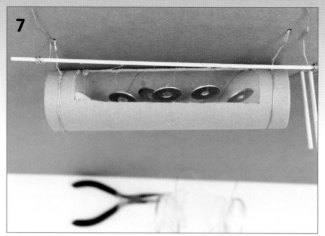

Step 7

Use wire and pliers to attach the paper towel roll to the base.

Step 8

A large metal funnel with a wide spout will make a loud sound when the marbles hit it.

Step 9

You can build musical instruments, such as a small xylophone, into your sonic art, too.

Step 10

With the help of an adult, create a narrow passage using nails so the marbles hit them as they go past.

Step 11

Finish your art with a finish line for the marbles. Try different materials to get a variety of sounds.

Step 12

Keep a pile of marbles handy and test each step as you make it to see if it works. When you've made all the steps, test the whole marble run. Change or add bits to fix any problems, and make sure it all runs smoothly.

Step 13.
When you're happy with your sonic art, you can make a video. Watch the marbles move from start to finish.

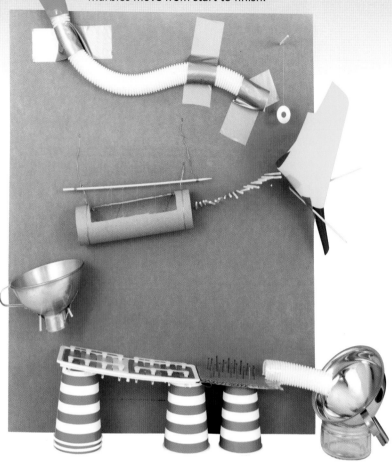

MILLIONS OF MARBLES

Many artists have played with marble runs as a form of art. Though a marble run can have lots parts, it's a very simple concept. It does not need electricity because it uses gravity to make the marble travel. Some artists use power to help the marbles move from the bottom and back to the top.

ART WITH SOUNDS

Sound art isn't a new invention. It goes back more than 100 years. Luigi Russolo (1885–1947), an Italian painter and musician, is usually said to be the first sound artist. He made machines that recreated the noises of everyday life. He called this the *Intonarumori*. Many artists since then have made sonic art, but it has become especially popular now. Computers and the Internet offer sound artists new ways to work.

INTRUDER ALERT!

Is someone trying to sneak into your room when you're not there? Catch them with this DIY electric pressure mat alarm.

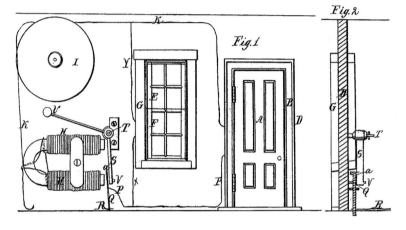

This diagram by Augustus Russell Pope shows how his invention worked.

AUGUSTUS RUSSELL POPE

(1819–1858)

Augustus Russell Pope was a church minister and inventor. In 1853, he had an idea for an electric alarm system. In this idea, movement at a door or window creates an **electric circuit**. This triggers the alarm and makes a bell ring.

Pope sold his ideas before he died, so another inventor created and sold his electric alarms. Before the electric alarm, people used guard dogs or hanging bells attached to a door.

> "To be applied to either a door or window, or both, of a dwelling-house or other building, for the purpose of giving alarm in case of burglarious or other attempts to enter through said door or window."
> – *Augustus Russell Pope*

WHAT YOU NEED

- two pieces of cardboard
- aluminum foil
- scissors
- tape
- insulated electrical wire
- wire cutters and strippers
- electrical tape
- a 9V battery
- a battery connector
- a small electric **buzzer**
- felt, thin foam, or rug underlay
- glue
- a door mat or rug

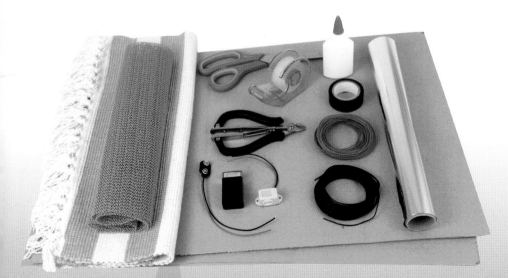

1

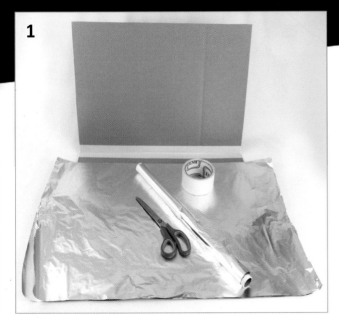

2

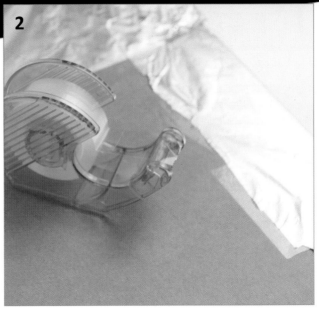

Step 1

Using tape, join the pieces of cardboard. This makes a folding pressure mat. Cut two pieces of aluminum foil that are slightly larger than the folded cardboard. Open up the cardboard and put one piece of foil on each side.

Step 2

Fold the foil over the outer edges of the cardboard. Hold the foil in place using tape. Stick the edges of the foil down with tape in the middle of the cardboard. Make sure the two pieces of foil do not touch.

3

4

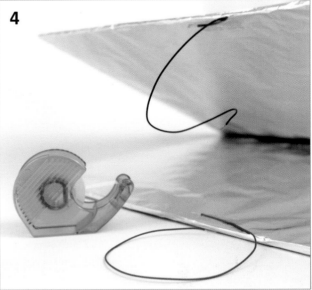

Step 3

With the help of an adult, cut two pieces of electrical wire. Each piece should be about 12 inches (30 cm) long. Use the wire strippers to strip about 0.39 inches (1 cm) of the plastic coating off both ends of each wire.

Step 4

Open out the cardboard and push one of the wire ends into the foil, near the outer edge. Hold it in place with tape, making sure the bare wire is touching the foil. Do the same with the second wire on the other side.

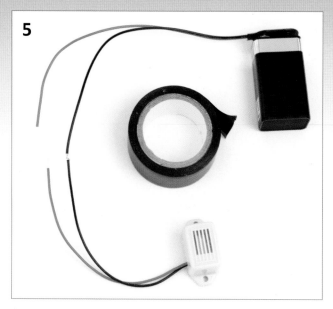

5

Step 5

Press the connector onto the battery. Attach the black wire on the connector to the black wire on the buzzer. You can attach them by twisting the bare ends together. Then firmly wrap them in electrical tape.

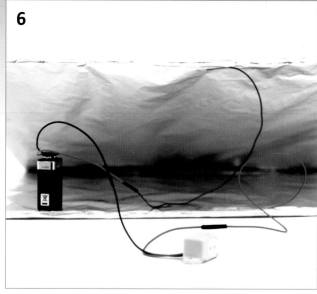

6

Step 6

Attach the free wire on the connector to the wire connected to one side of the mat. (You can attach it the same way you did in Step 5.) Then attach the free wire on the buzzer to the wire connected to the other side of the mat.

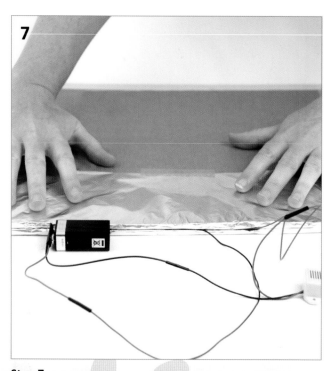

7

Step 7

Test your circuit. Press the two layers of foil together. This should complete the circuit and make a sound. (If it doesn't, check that your battery has power. Also check if all your connections are well attached.)

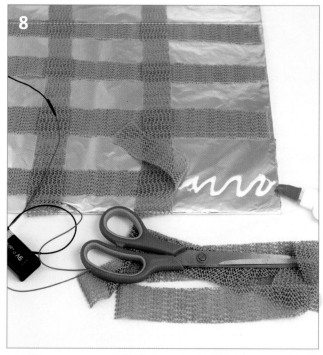

8

Step 8

Cut several strips of felt, thin foam, or underlay. These should be about 1 inch (2.5 cm) wide. Open out the pressure mat. Lay the strips in a grid pattern. Use a little glue to stick the strips in place and let it dry. Then trim the strips to the right length around the edges. This will help keep the two layers of foil apart until someone steps on the mat.

9

Step 9

Close the mat. Check that the foil does not touch and the buzzer does not sound. Hide the mat under a rug outside or inside of a doorway. The wires, battery, and buzzer should be out of sight. Now wait for someone to stand on the mat and listen to the buzzer go off!

CLOSING THE CIRCUIT

This alarm makes an electric circuit when the person tries to enter. Electric circuits can only work once all the parts of the circuit are together. This lets electricity from the battery flow through them. Standing on the mat connects the two pieces of foil and completes the circuit.

As the **electric current** moves through the buzzer, it travels around the wire. Remember, the wire is around a metal bar. When the current travels, it turns the bar into a magnet.

The magnet pulls towards a metal surface. This pattern makes a sound. When this happens, the circuit inside the buzzer breaks and turns the alarm off. Then the bar moves back and connects the circuit again. The bar moves back and forth, hitting the metal.

This idea can also work for automatic door systems. Instead of making an alarm, when someone steps on the mat, they open the door.

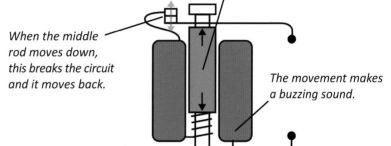

Electricity runs through the coil. Then, the rod in the middle becomes magnetic and it moves down.

When the middle rod moves down, this breaks the circuit and it moves back.

The movement makes a buzzing sound.

29

GLOSSARY

amplify To increase the power of a sound signal

buzzer An electric device that makes a buzzing sound

denser Having parts or molecules that are more closely packed together than another object

eidophone A device for using voice sound waves. This shows patterns for different notes.

electric circuit A loop of wires that an electric current can flow around

electric current A flow of electricity

energy The power to make things happen, move, or change

hydrophone A device for listening to sounds made underwater

installation A type of 3-D artwork made or installed into a particular space

Intonarumori A collection of sound art instruments. These were invented by Italian artist Luigi Russolo in the early 1900s.

loudspeakers Devices that change electrical signals into sounds loud enough to be heard at a distance

maracas A type of musical instrument made from a pair of hollow gourds or containers partly filled with beans, seeds, or other loose, hard materials that are shaken to make sounds

membrane A thin, flexible sheet of material, such as the eardrum or a drum skin

microphone A device that collects and turns sound waves into electric energy. This is used to record sound or make sound louder.

molecule The smallest particle of an object

percussion Describing musical instruments that make sounds by being struck or shaken

phonograph The name of the first sound recording and playback device. This was invented by Thomas Edison.

pitch How high or low a sound is

sonic To do with the nature of sound or sound waves

sound waves Waves made by energy as it travels through air, water, or any other solid or liquid

speakers Devices that turn an electrical signal into a sound you can hear

standing waves Vibrations of a surface that make some parts move and other parts stay still

ultrasound The use of sound waves and other vibrations to create a digital image

vibrate To move quickly and regularly back and forth

vibrations Continuous, quick, slight shaking movements

vinyl LP record A flat, circular piece of vinyl (a type of plastic) used to record sounds in LP (long-play) format

volume The loudness of a sound. This relates to the amount of energy in the vibrations it makes.

FURTHER INFORMATION

WEBSITES ABOUT SOUND

Exploratorium Science Snacks: Sound
www.exploratorium.edu/snacks/subject/sound

National Geographic Kids: The Science of Sound Videos
https://kids.nationalgeographic.com/explore/
youtube-playlist-pages/youtube-playlist-sound

Science Kids: Sound for Kids
www.sciencekids.co.nz/sound.html

Virtual Learning Commons: Light and Sound
http://vlc.ucdsb.ca/c.php?

WEBSITES ABOUT MAKING

Tate Kids: Make
www.tate.org.uk/kids/make

PBS Design Squad Global
http://pbskids.org/designsquad

Instructables
www.instructables.com

Teachers Try Science: Kids Experiments
www.teacherstryscience.org/
kids-experiments

WHERE TO BUY MATERIALS

Home Science Tools
www.homesciencetools.com

Staples
www.staples.com

The Home Depot
Tubing, wood, glue, and other hardware supplies
www.homedepot.com

BOOKS

Johnson, Robin. *How Does Sound Change?* Crabtree, 2014.

Johnson, Robin. *The Science of Sound Waves*. Crabtree, 2017.

Rooney, Anne. *Audio Engineering and the Science of Sound Waves*. Crabtree, 2014.

Spilsbury, Richard. *Investigating Sound*. Crabtree, 2018.

PLACES TO VISIT

The Tech Museum of Innovation
www.thetech.org

Exploratorium
www.exploratorium.edu

INDEX

AKB48 12
alarms 4–5, 26–29
art installations 4, 22–25
artists 4–5, 18–19, 22, 25

BBC Radiophonic
   Workshop 10
Bell, Alexander Graham 5
Biot, Jean-Baptiste 8
Blake, Lucien 16
bottle train 12–13

Derbyshire, Delia 10–11
dolphins 5

eardrums 4
ears, human 4–5, 11, 16–17
Edison, Thomas 20–21
eidophones 18–19

Glennie, Dame Evelyn 6–7

hearing 4–5, 7, 11,
   16–17, 21
Hughes, Megan
   Watts 18–19
hydrophones 16–17

instruments, musical
   4, 6–7, 10–14, 24

Kircher, Athanasius 14

Leuschner, Dirk 22

Maxwell, Kym 22
music 4–7, 10–15, 18–19
musicians 6–7, 10–11,
   18–19, 25

percussion 6–7
phonographs 20–21
Pope, Augustus
   Russell 26, 29
pressure mat alarm 26–29

radiophonic sound 10–11
record players 20–21
recording sounds 5,
   10–11, 20–21
Rossolo, Luigi 25

singing 4–5, 7, 12, 17–19
sonar 5
sonic art 5, 22–25
sonic marble run 22–25
sound effects 5, 10–11
sound patterns 18–19
speakers 5, 9, 14–15

speaking tubes 8–9

telephones 5, 8

underwater sounds
   4–5, 16–17

vibrations 4–5, 7, 9,
   11, 13, 15, 17–22
vinyl records 20–21

waves, sound 4, 5,
   9, 17–19, 21
whales 16–17